The Making of the Constitution

by
Gordon S. Wood

THE NINTH

Charles Edmondson Historical Lectures

Baylor University • Waco, Texas
March 25 and 26, 1987

MARKHAM PRESS FUND
WACO, TEXAS

This volume is the twenty-first volume published by the Markham Press Fund of Baylor University Press, established in memory of Dr. L. N. and Princess Finch Markham of Longview, Texas, by their daughters, Mrs. R. Matt Dawson of Waco, Texas, and Mrs. B. Reid Clanton of Longview, Texas.

The Charles Edmondson Historical Lecture Series, Number 9.

Rufus B. Spain, general editor

Publication of this series of lectures is made possible by a special grant from Dr. E. Bud Edmondson of Longview, Texas.

Library of Congress Catalog Card Number: 87-73124
International Standard Book Number: 0-918954-54-1

Printed in the United States of America by the Baylor University Printing Service, Waco, Texas 76798.

This book was set in Hanover, and was printed and bound by Baylor University.

FOREWORD

In 1975 Dr. E. Bud Edmondson of Longview, Texas, began an endowment fund at Baylor University to honor his father, Mr. Charles S. B. Edmondson. Dr. Edmondson's intent was to have the proceeds from the fund used to bring to the University outstanding historians who could synthesize, interpret, and communicate history in such a way as to make the past relevant to the present generation.

Baylor University and the Waco community are grateful to Dr. Edmondson for his generosity in establishing the CHARLES EDMONDSON HISTORICAL LECTURES.

Dr. Gordon S. Wood, the ninth Edmondson Lecturer, presents important information about the founding period in our nation's history, conveying not only the content but also the spirit of the debates surrounding the Philadelphia convention and its aftermath. Lecture I concerns the origins of the Constitution, and Lecture II focuses on the convention and ratification.

****

The views expressed in these lectures are those of the author and do not necessarily reflect the position of Baylor University or of the Markham Press Fund.

****

Although the Charles Edmondson Historical Lectures have been presented annually at Baylor University since 1978, they have not always been available for publication by the Markham Press Fund. Therefore, while this volume represents the sixth of the lectures to be published, they were the ninth presented in the lecture series. A list of previous lectures appears at the end of this work.

Earlier versions of these lectures were presented as the Samuel Paley Lectures in American Culture and Civilization, The Hebrew University of Jerusalem, January 6, 13, 1987.

3

THE ORIGINS OF THE CONSTITUTION

During these Bicentennial celebrations historians are going to have to work hard to convince their fellow Americans of the extraordinary and unanticipated character of the Constitution of 1787. We tend to take the Constitution and a strong national government very much for granted. We take them so much for granted in fact that we tend to collapse the time between the Declaration of Independence and the actual writing of the Constitution a decade later. We wonder why Americans in 1776 did not go at once to the Constitution. Why did they even bother with the Articles of Confederation? Was not the United States destined to be an integrated nation with a powerful central government?

It may look that way from the vantage point of the late twentieth century, but from the vantage point of 1776 a strong central government such as the Constitution created did not look inevitable at all. At the time of the Declaration of Independence no American even contemplated the kind of strong national government that was formed a mere decade later. The American colonists had had too much despairing experience with the far-removed governmental power of the British empire to think about erecting a strong distant government for themselves. If they had learned anything under the empire it was that the closer the government was to the people, the more local the government, the safer and less tyrannical it was likely to be. Besides, the best minds of the eighteenth century, including Montesquieu, had repeatedly told the world that a republic could exist only in a small territory. A monarchy with its centralized authority and its hierarchical social ligaments and its standing army could maintain itself over a large heterogeneous population. But a republic which depended on consent from below, from the people, needed a small homogeneous population.

Too many diverse interests and a republic would fly apart. Therefore it was natural and inevitable that Americans in 1776 would create separate independent republics tied together only in a confederation or alliance. At the moment of Revolution the Articles of Confederation, proposed by the Continental Congress in 1777, were about as far as most Americans were willing to go in creating a central government.

The Articles were an alliance of thirteen sovereign states, a binding together of separate states in a manner not all that different from the present-day European community of nation-states. Each state had separate and equal representation in the Confederation Congress, and no changes could be made in the Articles without the agreement of every state. Although this Confederation was given some substantial powers concerning war and diplomacy, the borrowing of money, and the requisition of troops, it lacked the crucial authority to tax and to regulate the commerce of the United States. Indeed, all final lawmaking authority remained with the individual states. Congressional resolutions were merely recommendations to be left to the states to enforce. The Confederation had no real executive or judicial authority. To remove any doubts of the decentralized nature of this Confederation, Article 2 of our first national constitution stated bluntly that "each State retains its sovereignty, freedom and independence, and every power jurisdiction, and right, which is not by this confederation expressly delegated to the United States, in Congress assembled." The Confederation was less a national constitution than it was a treaty among independent states. It was intended to be and remained, as Article 3 declared, "a firm league of friendship" among states very jealous of their individual sovereignty.

The Confederation achieved a good deal, including the winning of the war and independence from Great Britain and the organizing of the new territories in the West. But scarcely a half-dozen years after their final ratification by all thirteen states in 1781, the Articles were virtually moribund, and nearly all Americans were calling for their amendment. The Confederation was not adequate, it seemed, to the problems of the 1780s; a more powerful central government was apparently needed. The calling of the Philadelphia Convention in 1787 and the new Constitution were the results.

What had happened? What could have occurred since 1776 to change American thinking so dramatically? What on earth could have forced them to put aside their earlier fears of far-removed central power and to create such a strong national government as the Constitution provided for? For the new government was not merely a stronger league of friendship with a few new powers granted to the Congress. It was a radically new government altogether—one that utterly transformed the structure of central authority and greatly diminished the power of the several states. The Constitution of 1787 created a national republic in its own right operating directly on individuals over half a continent. It created in fact what a decade earlier in 1776 had seemed theoretically impossible and virtually inconceivable. Explaining the Constitution is no easy matter. It was not as inevitable as it may seem to us today.

Nineteenth-century Americans tended to explain the writing of the Constitution in heroic terms. John Fiske, in a book published in 1888 for the centennial celebration of the Constitution, *The Critical Period of American History*, summed up this nineteenth-century thinking. "It is not too much to say," he wrote, "that the period of five years following the peace of 1783 was the most critical moment in all the history of the American people."[1] Fiske pictured the 1780s as a time of chaos and anarchy with the country's finances near ruin. The Confederation government was collapsing, and the various state governments, beset by debtor and paper money advocates who were pressing creditor and commercial interests to the wall, were flying off in separate directions. It was a desperate situation retrieved only at the eleventh hour by the high-minded intervention of the Founding Fathers. These few great men saved the country from disaster.

The problem with this dominant nineteenth-century interpretation is that there does not appear to have been any near-collapse of the economy or society. There was no anarchy, no financial crisis, apparently no real "critical period" after all. Historical studies of the twentieth century have tended to minimize the criticalness of the 1780s. Things seem not to have been as bad as the Federalists or Fiske pictured them. This has been the thrust of the work of the twentieth-century Progressive and neo-Progressive historians—beginning with

Charles Beard at the beginning of the century and extending up into our own time with Merrill Jensen, James Ferguson, and Jackson Turner Main. "Clearly," writes Ferguson, "it was not the era of public bankruptcy and currency depreciation that historians used to depict."[2] Both the Confederation and the state governments had done much to stabilize finances in the aftermath of the Revolution. The states had already moved to assume payment of the public debt, and the deficits were not really that serious. There was, to be sure, economic dislocation and unsettlement, but there was no collapse of the economy. There was a depression in 1784-85, but by 1786 the country was coming out of it, and many Federalists were aware of the returning prosperity. The commercial outlook was far from bleak. Americans were freely trading with each other and were reaching out to ports throughout the world—to the West Indies and Spanish America, to the continent of Europe, to Alaska, to Russia, and even to China.

The 1780s were in fact a time of great excitement and exuberance. The country was bursting with energy and enterprise, and people were multiplying and were on the move. They were spilling over the mountains into the new western areas with astonishing rapidity. Kentucky, which had virtually no white Americans at the time of Independence, already by 1780 had 20,000. Despite a slackening of immigration and the loss of tens of thousands of loyalists, the population grew as never before or since. The 1780s saw the fastest rate of population growth of any decade in American history. This was merely one measure of the high expectations and exuberance of the period. There were economic problems of course, "but," as Jensen writes, "there is no evidence of stagnation and decay in the 1780s." In fact, says Jensen, "the period was one of extraordinary economic growth."[3] The promises of the Revolution were being fulfilled for the bulk of the society. The pursuit of happiness had real meaning for countless individuals.

If all this is true, then why did Americans create the Constitution? If the Confederation was not doing too bad a job and economic conditions in the 1780s were not desperate, then why did something as extraordinary and unanticipated as the Constitution have to be written?

The questions are not easily answered. In fact, the difficulty of answering them led the Progressive and neo-Progressive historians to picture the move for the Constitution as something of a fraud. The creation of the Constitution, they suggested, was the work of a tightly organized minority of continental-minded men who wished to reverse the democratic tendencies of the Revolution. The Constitution was a response out of all proportion to the social and economic reality of the time. The critical period, wrote Charles Beard, was perhaps not so critical after all, "but a phantom of the imagination produced by some undoubted evils which could have been remedied without a political revolution."[4] The Federalist conservatives therefore had to exaggerate the anarchical conditions of the 1780s in order to justify the making of the Constitution. A sense of crisis, writes Main, had to be "conjured up" when "actually the country faced no such emergency."[5]

Charles Beard's famous book *An Economic Interpretation of the Constitution* (1913) was the foundation stone of this argument. Beard saw the Constitution as something foisted on the country by a minority with particular property interests to protect against rampaging democratic state legislatures. Although his particular arguments and proofs have been torn to shreds and are too crudely presented to be persuasive today, his book dominated the historical literature on the Constitution for a half-century or so, and it still casts a long shadow over writing about the Constitution. For all of Beard's errors and crudities, his belief that something was happening in 1787 other than a mere heroic rescue of the country by a group of great men has had a stimulating effect on our historical investigations of the origins of the Constitution. After Beard, a straightforward Federalist explanation of the Constitution in the manner of John Fiske could no longer be persuasive. But neither can a straightforward Beardian interpretation of the Constitution by itself be convincing. Together, however, both arguments may add up to a satisfying explanation of the making of the Constitution in 1787.

There are actually two levels of explanation for the Constitution, two different sets of problems, two distinct reform movements in the 1780s that eventually came together to form the Convention of 1787. One operated at the national level and involved problems of the Articles of Confederation. The other

9

operated at the state level and involved problems in the state legislatures. The national problems account for the ready willingness of people in 1786-87 to accede to the convening of delegates at Philadelphia. But the state problems, problems that went to the heart of America's experiment in republicanism, account for the radical and unprecedented nature of the federal government created in Philadelphia.

The weaknesses of the Articles of Confederation were evident early, even before the Articles were formally ratified by all the states in 1781. By 1780 the war was dragging on longer than anyone had expected, and the skyrocketing inflation of the paper money that was being used to finance it was unsettling commerce and business. The Articles barred congressional delegates from serving more than three years in any six-year period, and leadership in the Confederation was changeable and confused. The states were ignoring congressional resolutions and were refusing to supply their allotted contributions to the central government. The Congress stopped paying interest on the public debt. The Continental army was smoldering with resentment at the lack of pay and was falling apart through desertions and even outbreaks of mutiny. By early 1781 the Confederation Congress could not even afford the cost of printing its own proceedings. All of these circumstances were forcing various groups and interests to seek to add to the powers of the Congress.

The first of these interests was the officer corps of the army. After the victory at Yorktown in October 1781 and the opening of peace negotiations with Great Britain, some of the army officers became desperate. The prospect that Congress might demobilize the army without fulfilling its promises of back pay and pensions created a crisis that brought the United States as close to a military coup d'état as it has ever been. In March 1783 the officers of Washington's army, encamped at Newburgh on the Hudson River, issued an address to the Congress concerning their pay, and actually considered some sort of military action against the Confederation. Only when Washington personally intervened and refused to support a movement that was designed, he said, "to open the floodgates of civil discord, and deluge our rising empire in blood," was the crisis averted.[6] In the aftermath of the Newburgh incident the officers formed a hereditary institution designed to commemorate their achievements in the Revolutionary War. They called their society the Order of the Cincinnati, named after the legendary Roman republican leader Cincinnatus, who retired from war to take up his plow. Although Washington became the president of the organization, the Cincinnati aroused bitter hostility in the country from those who thought this was the first step toward establishing an hereditary aristocracy in America. This ferocious criticism forced the army officers to deny some of their pretensions, and the Cincinnati soon became simply one pressure group among others lobbying for a stronger central government.

A second interest working towards strengthening the Confederation government were the public creditors, those who held federal bonds and loan certificates. If the Confederation were unable even to pay interest on its debts there was no possibility of the Congress's borrowing more money. No one saw this more clearly than did Robert Morris, the wealthy Philadelphia merchant who became superintendent of finance and virtual head of the Confederation in 1781. Morris envisioned a financial program that anticipated Hamilton's of a decade later. He sought to stabilize the economy, to establish a bank, and to involve financial and commercial groups with the central government. Crucial to his plans for making the federal government's bonds more secure for investors was amending the Articles so as to grant the Confederation the power to levy a 5 per cent duty on imports. First Rhode Island and later New York refused to give the unanimous consent of the states necessary for amending the Articles. Despite this frustration, however, by 1786 momentum was building to give at least some sort of taxing power to the Confederation government.

A third interest behind strengthening the Confederation involved commerce. A number of groups in the 1780s became increasingly eager to grant to the Congress the power to regulate international trade. Merchants with interstate connections, southern planters interested in compelling the opening of foreign markets for their agricultural staples, and urban artisans desirous of tariff protection against competitive European manufactures—all for different motives wanted Congress to have the authority to pass navigation laws, to levy tariffs, and

11

to retaliate against the British mercantilist system. State and sectional jealousies blocked several attempts to grant the Congress a restricted power over commerce, but, as in the case of the taxing power, momentum by 1786 was pointing toward some sort of commercial regulatory power being added to Congress's authority. At a meeting at Mount Vernon in 1785 Virginia and Maryland resolved a number of disputes concerning the navigation of Chesapeake Bay and the Potomac River. This conference suggested the advantages of reforming the Confederation outside of Congress itself and led to Virginia's invitation to the states to meet at Annapolis in 1786 "to consider and recommend a federal plan for regulating commerce." In just this way did problems of commerce move the country toward reforming the Articles.

A fourth area of national concern lay in foreign affairs. By the mid-80s a number of important American leaders were angry at the ways the new confederated republic, the United States, was being humiliated in the world. Since American ships now lacked the protection of the British flag many of them were seized by corsairs from the Muslim states of North Africa, and their crews sold as slaves. The Congress had no money to pay the necessary tribute and ransoms to these Barbary pirates. In the late-eighteenth-century world of hostile empires, it was even difficult for the new republican confederacy to maintain its territorial integrity. Britain refused to send a diplomatic minister to the United States and ignored its treaty obligations to evacuate its military posts in the Northwest, claiming that the United States had not honored its own commitments. The treaty of peace had specified that the Confederation would recommend to the states that loyalist property that had been confiscated during the Revolution be restored, and that neither side would make laws obstructing the recovery of pre-war debts. When the states flouted these treaty obligations, the impotent Confederation could do nothing; and therefore British troops remained in Detroit, Niagara, Oswego and other posts within American territory.

Britain was known to be plotting with the Indians and encouraging separatist movements in the Northwest and in the Vermont borderlands, and Spain was doing the same in the Southwest. Spain in fact refused to recognize American claims to the territory between the Ohio River and Florida. In 1784, in an effort to influence American settlers moving into Kentucky and Tennessee, Spain closed the Mississippi River to American trade. Many of the Westerners were ready to deal with any government that could ensure access to the sea for their agricultural produce. As Washington noted in 1784, they were "on a pivot. The touch of a feather would turn them any way."[7] Thus began the so-called "Spanish conspiracy" that eventually involved Spanish payments of money to several high officials of the American government, including Senator Blount of Tennessee and James Wilkinson, the eventual commander-in-chief of the American army. The intrigue eventually came to a head with Aaron Burr's abortive plot in 1806-07 either to attack Mexico or to separate the western area from the United States.

In 1785-86, John Jay, a New Yorker and the secretary of foreign affairs, negotiated a treaty with the Spanish minister to the United States, Diego de Gardoqui. By the terms of this agreement, Spain was opened to American trade in return for America's renunciation of its right to navigate the Mississippi for several decades. Out of fear of being denied an outlet to the sea in the West, the southern states prevented the necessary nine-state majority in the Congress from agreeing to the treaty. But the willingness of seven states to sacrifice western interests for the sake of northern merchants aroused long-existing sectional jealousies and threatened to shatter the Union. In an address to the Congress in August 1786 Jay defended his treaty on the grounds that it was the best the United States could get from Spain, at least until it "shall become more really and truly a nation than it at present is."[8] To some Americans it seemed that unless something were done soon the United States would break apart into two or three separate confederations.

By 1786 these various interests and pressures were mounting, and some sort of reform of the Articles seemed inevitable. Everywhere American leaders, even those who would later oppose the Constitution of 1787, acknowledged the necessity of adding some powers to the Confederation Congress. Though James Madison had his pessimism about what could be done at the Annapolis meeting in 1786 confirmed by the fact that only five states showed up, the national mood was increasingly receptive to some sort of reform of the national government. After only two days of discussion the Annapolis delegates issued a report in September 1786 drafted by Hamilton requesting the states to elect delegates to a second convention to be held in Philadelphia on the second Monday in May of 1787 "to devise such further provisions as shall appear to them necessary to render the constitution of the Federal Government adequate to the exigencies of the Union."[9]

By this time most Americans were prepared for some additional powers being added to the Congress, and even later opponents of the Constitution were remarkably casual about the coming convention in Philadelphia.

Although by 1787 nearly all of America's political leaders agreed that some reform of the Articles was necessary, few expected what the Philadelphia Convention eventually created. For the new national government framed in 1787 went way beyond what the weaknesses of the Articles demanded. Granting the Congress the authority to raise revenue, to regulate trade, to pay off its debts, and to deal effectively in international affairs did not require the total scrapping of the Articles and the formation of an extraordinarily powerful and distant national government the like of which was beyond anyone's imagination a decade earlier. The new Constitution of 1787 therefore cannot be explained by the obvious and generally acknowledged defects of the Articles of Confederation. Something else more fundamental than the problems of credit, commerce, and foreign policy lay behind the Constitution of 1787.

To understand the proposal written by James Madison that became the working model of the Convention—the so-called Virginia Plan—and the resultant Constitution, we have to go to another deeper level of explanation than that of the central government. We have to go to problems within the states themselves. It is ultimately these state political problems that best explain the origins of the Constitution.

By the mid-1780s a number of American leaders had become deeply alarmed by what had happened in the states. In 1776 the Revolutionaries had placed great confidence in the ability of the state legislatures to promote the public good and protect the people's liberties. In their Revolutionary state constitutions

14

written in 1776-77 Americans had greatly increased the size of the state legislatures, had made them more representative of the people than the colonial assemblies had been, and had granted enormous power to them. But in the years after 1776 the state legislatures did not live up to the Revolutionaries' initial expectations. The Revolution unleashed acquisitive and factional economic interests that no one had quite realized existed in American society, and these partial factional interests were now demanding and getting protection and satisfaction from state legislatures that were elected annually (an innovation in most states) by the broadest electorates in the world. Everywhere in the states electioneering and the open competition for office increased, and new petty uneducated entrepreneurs like Abraham Yates, a part-time lawyer and shoemaker of Albany, and William Findley, a Scotch-Irish ex-weaver of western Pennsylvania, used popular electoral appeals to vault into political leadership in the state legislatures.

No one in the 1780s saw what was happening more clearly than did James Madison. In the winter of 1786-87 he put his ideas together in a working paper that he called the "vices of the political system of the United States." In this paper, which was the most important document dealing with American constitutionalism written between the Articles of Confederation and the federal Constitution, Madison spent very little time on the weaknesses of the Confederation. Instead he concentrated on the deficiences of the state governments, what he called the "multiplicity," "mutability," and "injustice" of the laws passed by the states.[10] Particularly alarming in his eyes were the paper money acts, stay laws, and other forms of debtor relief legislation that hurt creditors and violated individual property rights. The states were the real source of the "vices" of the American political system. Even the impotence of the Confederation could be laid at the door of the state legislators.

Madison did not come to these ideas from reading all those bundles of books that Jefferson was sending him from Europe. He learned about the vices of state legislative politics from first-hand experience—by being a member of the Virginia assembly. During the years 1784 through 1787 Madison attended four sessions of the Virginia legislature. This was a frustrating and disillusioning experience for Madison, for he found out really

15

for the first time what democracy might mean in America.

Although Madison in these years had some notable legislative achievements, particularly with his shepherding into enactment Jefferson's famous bill for religious freedom, he was continually exasperated by what Jefferson years later (no doubt following Madison's own account) referred to as "the endless quibbles, chicaneries, perversions, vexations, and delays of lawyers and demi-lawyers" in the assembly.[11] The legislators seemed so small-minded, so parochial, so illiberal. They rarely had any regard for public honor or honesty, and always seemed to have only "a particular interest to serve" regardless of the needs of the whole state or the nation. They often made a travesty of the legislative process and were reluctant to do anything that might appear unpopular with their constituents. They postponed taxes, subverted debts owed to the subjects of Great Britain, and passed, defeated, and repassed bills in the most haphazard ways. Most of his and Jefferson's plans for legal and court reform were lost in a sea of localism. "Important bills prepared at leisure by skilful hands," he complained, were mauled and torn apart by "crudeness and tedious discussion." He repeatedly found himself having to beat back the "itch for paper money" and other measures "of a popular cast." Too often he had to admit that the only hope he had was "of moderating the fury," not defeating it.

It was not what republican lawmaking was supposed to be. Madison continually had to make concessions to the "prevailing sentiments," whether or not such sentiments promoted the good of the state or nation. He had to agree to bad laws for fear of getting worse ones, or give up good bills "rather than pay such a price" as opponents wanted. Today legislators are used to this sort of political horse-trading. But Madison simply was not yet ready for the logrolling and the pork barreling that would eventually become the staples of American legislative politics. By 1786 he knew that appealing to the people had none of the beneficial effects good republicans had expected. A bill having to do with court reform was, for example, "to be printed for consideration of the public"; but "instead of calling forth the sanction of the wise & virtuous" this action, Madison feared, would only "be a signal to interested men to redouble their efforts to get into the Legislature."[12] Democracy was no solution to the problem; democracy was the problem.

It was not just that the state legislators themselves were bad. More alarming was the fact that such legislators were only reflecting the particular interests and parochial outlooks of their constituents. Too many of the American people could not see beyond their own pocketbooks or their own neighborhoods. "Individuals of extended views, and of national pride," said Madison, might be able to bring public proceedings to an enlightened cosmopolitan standard, but their example could never be followed by "the multitude." "Is it to be imagined that an ordinary citizen or even an assembly-man of R. Island in estimating the policy of paper money, ever considered or cared in what light the measure would be viewed in France or Holland; or even in Massachusetts or Connecticut? It was a sufficient temptation to both that it was for their interest." And in a republican government where "the majority however composed, ultimately give the law," what was to restrain these selfish interested majorities "from unjust violations of the rights and interests of the minority, or of individuals."[13]

Madison's experience with the populist politics of the state legislatures was not unusual; indeed, he could never have gained support for his reform proposals if it had been. Others too in the 1780s were baffled by the chaos of law-making in the states. Laws, as the Vermont Council of Censors said in 1786, were "altered—realtered—made better—made worse, and kept in such a fluctuating position that persons in civil commissions scarce know what is law."[14] In fact, Madison believed that more laws were enacted by the states in the decade following Independence than in the entire colonial period—all as a result of the rapid turnover of seats and the scrambling among different shifting narrow interests in the society. Everywhere localism seemed to be swallowing up the state and national good. In all the states the representatives, noted Ezra Stiles, president of Yale College, were concerned with only the special interests of their electors. Whenever a bill was read in the legislature, "every one instantly thinks how it will affect his constituents."[15] Such pandering to voters was not what many Americans had expected from the Revolution.

By the mid-1780s many American leaders were convinced that the state legislatures and majority factions within those legislatures were the greatest source of tyranny in America. At the time of Independence none of the Revolutionaries had expected such majoritarian tyranny. Although some tories had warned that the people were quite capable of tyranny, whigs had dismissed such fears out of hand. The people, who loved liberty, could not tyrannize over themselves. The idea, said John Adams in 1775, was illogical: "a democratical despotism is a contradiction in terms."[16] But experience since the Revolution had taught American leaders differently. Legislatures, however representative, however popularly elected, were quite capable of tyranny. It did not matter, wrote Jefferson, that such legislative representatives were numerous: "173 despots would surely be as oppressive as one." Nor did it matter that such representatives were chosen by the people: "An elective *despotism* was not the government we fought for."[17]

Such legislative abuses were not like the deficiencies of the Confederation. They were not something that simply caused vexation, inconvenience, or embarrassment. Nor were they easily remedied. For such legislative abuses struck at the heart of what the Revolution was about. They, said Madison, "brought into question the fundamental principle of republican Government, that the majority who rule in such governments are the safest Guardians both of public Good and private rights."[18]

At first leaders responded to these problems of state legislative tyranny by proposing changes in the state governments and state constitutions. Reformers sought to take back some of the powers that had been given to the state legislatures, particularly the lower houses of representatives, by the Revolutionary state constitutions in 1776-77. They tried to strengthen the senates, the governors, and the judiciaries and to reduce the democratic nature of the state governments. Such reformers were most successful with the Massachusetts constitution of 1780. The constitution gave the governor an extraordinary degree of power, including the power of appointment and a limited veto over all legislation. Such a conservative constitution formed a model for others of what state reformers in the 1780s should aim for.

Thus when a rebellion of nearly 2000 debtor farmers led by a former militia captain, Daniel Shays, broke out in western

Massachusetts in late 1786, many leaders were surprised. But more alarming than the rebellion itself was the fact that Shays' sympathizers were getting elected to the Massachusetts legislature and enacting into law debtor relief legislation that they could not get by coercively closing courts. Such action led some Americans to believe that "sedition itself will sometimes make laws."[19]

Even before Shays' Rebellion convinced many that relief from popular pressures could not be found in the model constitution of Massachusetts, other Americans were looking beyond the state level for a remedy to these political problems within the states.

By 1786-87 America saw a coming together of two different and hitherto separate reform movements. It was not just that the Confederation Congress had to be saved from the states but that the states had to be saved from themselves. All those groups and interests that had long been concerned with strengthening the Articles—former army officers, public creditors, merchants, Southern planters, artisans, diplomatic officials—were now joined by many American leaders deeply disturbed by popular politics and majoritarian factionalism within the states. This growing distress over state politics now overwhelmed the state particularism and the jealousy and fear of far-removed central power that had hitherto inhibited reform of the national government. Many Americans were no longer merely interested in modifying the Articles of Confederation. Many of the delegates to the Philadelphia Convention were eager to weaken if not destroy the states and the democratic excesses they had brought forth. "The vile State governments are the sources of pollution, which will contaminate the American name for ages. . . . Smite them," Henry Knox urged Rufus King who was attending the Philadelphia Convention, "smite them, in the name of God and the people."[20]

By 1787 the terms of the problem facing America had been recast. It was no longer merely a matter of strengthening the union or standing tall in foreign affairs or satisfying particular creditor, commercial, or artisan interests. Because the states in 1776 had been the arena where the Revolutionary experiment in popular government was to be tested, the stakes were as high as they ever have been. The convention was meeting not simply to reform the Articles of Confederation, but, said Madison, to "decide forever the fate of republican government."[21]

NOTES FOR LECTURE I

1. John Fiske, *The Critical Period of American History* (Boston: Houghton, Mifflin and Company, 1888), 55.
2. E. James Ferguson, *The Power of the Purse: A History of American Public Finance, 1776-1790* (Chapel Hill: University of North Carolina Press, 1961), 337.
3. Merrill Jensen, *The New Nation: A History of the United States, 1781-1789* (New York: Alfred A. Knopf, 1950), 423, 424.
4. Charles Beard, *An Economic Interpretation of the Constitution of the United States* (New York: Macmillan, 1935), 48.
5. Jackson Turner Main, *The Antifederalists: Critics of the Constitution, 1781-1788* (Chapel Hill: University of North Carolina Press, 1961), 177-178.
6. James Thomas Flexner, *George Washington in the American Revolution (1775-1783)* (Boston: Little, Brown, 1968), 507.
7. Washington to Governor Benjamin Harrison, 10 October 1784, in John C. Fitzpatrick, ed., *The Writings of George Washington* (Washington, D.C.: U.S. Government Printing Office, 1938), XXVII, 475.
8. John Jay, "Address Before Congress on Spanish-American Diplomacy, August 3, 1786," in Ruhl J. Bartlett, ed., *The Record of American Diplomacy* (New York: A. A. Knopf, 1952), 56.
9. Report of Annapolis Convention, September 14, 1786, in Jack P. Greene, ed., *Colonies to Nation, 1763-1789: A Documentary History of the American Revolution* (New York: Norton, 1975), 511.
10. James Madison, "Vices of the Political System of the United States," in William T. Hutchinson et al., eds., *The Papers of James Madison* (Chicago: University of Chicago Press, 1962-), IX, 346.
11. Jefferson quoted in Ralph Ketcham, *James Madison: A Biography* (New York: Macmillan, 1971), 162.

12. Drew R. McCoy, "The Virginia Port Bill of 1784," *Virginia Magazine of History and Biography*, v. 83 (1975), 294, 292; Madison to Edmund Pendleton 9 January 1787, to Thomas Jefferson, 4 December 1786, to George Washington, 24 December 1786, 7 December 1786, in Hutchinson *et al.*, eds. *Papers of Madison*, IX, 244, 191, 225, 200.
13. Madison, "Vices," Hutchinson *et al.*, eds., *Papers of Madison*, IX, 354, 355-56.
14. "Address of the Council of Censors," February 14, 1786, William Slade, ed., *Vermont State Papers* (Middlebury, Vermont, 1823), 540.
15. Stiles, quoted in Gordon S. Wood, *The Creation of the American Republic, 1776-1787* (Chapel Hill: University of North Carolina Press, 1969), 195.
16. John Adams, "Novanglus" (1775), in Charles Francis Adams, ed., *The Works of John Adams* (Boston: Hews and Goss, 1850-56), IV, 79.
17. Thomas Jefferson, *Notes on the State of Virginia*, ed., William Peden (Chapel Hill: University of North Carolina Press, 1955), 120.
18. Madison, quoted in Wood, *Creation of American Republic*, 140.
19. Boston *Independent Chronicle*, May 10, 1787.
20. Knox, quoted in William Winslow Crosskey and William Jeffrey, Jr., *Politics and the Constitution in the History of the United States* (Chicago: University of Chicago Press, 1980), III, 420-421.
21. Madison, quoted in Charles Warren, *The Making of the Constitution* (Cambridge, Massachusetts: Harvard University Press, 1947), 82.

THE CONVENTION
AND RATIFICATION

By 1787 almost all Americans agreed that something had to be done about reforming the central government. Even if the Philadelphia Convention had not met and drafted a new Constitution when it did, some sort of amendment of the Articles of Confederation would sooner or later have occurred. Nearly everyone now agreed that some additional powers, namely the powers to tax and to regulate commerce, would have to be granted to the Confederation Congress. An impotent league of states was no longer adequate to the exigencies facing the union. People were prepared for the Philadelphia Convention to do something.

But the federal Constitution that came out of the Convention was not what most people had expected. The Constitution went way beyond a mere amendment of the Articles, way beyond simply strengthening the Confederation. It marked a wholesale revolution in American government. It created a national continental republic operating directly on individuals where none had existed before. The new central government was no longer a league of independent states but a republican government in its own right—an extraordinarily powerful distant government that threatened to overawe the separate states. It was the sort of central government that had been unthinkable ten years earlier, and it stunned many Americans, including those who had expected the Philadelphia Convention to do something about the Articles. Had Americans known beforehand what the Convention would do, "probably no state," said "The Federal Farmer," "would have appointed members to the convention. . . . Probably not one man in ten thousand in the United States . . . had an idea that the old ship was to be destroyed."[1]

Startling as it was, however, the Constitution that emerged

from the Convention in September of 1787 was not the half of it. If those who were surprised at the power of the national government created by the Constitution had known what actually had gone on in the Convention, they would have been even more shocked. For the national government that came out of the Convention was much less powerful than many of the delegates had wanted. The Constitution was a compromise; indeed, in the eyes of some of the leading delegates, including James Madison, it was a failure, inadequate to the crisis facing the nation and probably doomed to destruction. Three and a half months of deliberation at Philadelphia had forced concessions and changes and had created something that no one had anticipated.

Fifty-five delegates representing twelve states attended the Philadelphia Convention in the summer of 1787, from May 14 to September 18. Rhode Island, which feared any national regulation of its trade or its paper money, refused to have anything to do with efforts to revise the Articles. Not that anyone cared. One Boston newspaper described Rhode Island's absence as "a joyous" rather than a "grievous" occasion. For Madison, as for many others, Rhode Island represented all that he hated in state popular politics and majoritarian factionalism in the 1780s. "Nothing can exceed the wickedness and folly which continue to rule there," wrote Madison. "All sense of Character as well as Right have been obliterated."[2] Although many of the delegates were young men—their average age was forty-two—most were well educated and experienced members of America's political elite. Thirty-nine had served in the Congress at one time or another, eight had worked in the state constitutional conventions, seven had been state governors, and thirty-four were lawyers. One-third were veterans of the Continental army, that great dissolvent of state loyalties, as Washington described it.[3] Nearly all were gentlemen, "natural aristocrats," who took their political superiority for granted as an inevitable consequence of their social and economic position. The Convention chose Washington as its president. But some of the outstanding figures of the Revolution were not present: Samuel Adams was ill; Thomas Jefferson and John Adams were serving as ministers abroad; and Richard Henry Lee and Patrick Henry, although selected by the Virginia legislature, refused to attend the Convention. "I smelt a Rat," said Henry.[4] The most influential delegations were those of Pennsylvania and Virginia, which included Gouverneur Morris and James Wilson of Pennsylvania, and Edmund Randolph, George Mason, and James Madison of Virginia.

The Convention was supposed to begin on May 14, but not until May 25 was a quorum of states present and not until May 29 did the Convention get down to serious business. The delegates immediately took extraordinary steps to keep their proceedings secret: no copies of anything in their journal were allowed, nothing said in the Convention was to be communicated to the outside society, and sentries were even posted to keep out intruders. This sensitivity to the public out-of-doors was new; no such decisions concerning secrecy had been taken in the state constitutional conventions a decade earlier. But in the intervening time many leaders had discovered that there were emerging popular spokesmen everywhere eager to pounce on anything that might discredit established elite leaders. If the Convention's deliberations were likely to be picked up by "imprudent printers" and conveyed to "the too credulous and unthinking mobility," then the delegates' freedom to discuss issues openly and candidly would be seriously inhibited. Madison later reportedly declared that "no Constitution would ever have been adopted by the convention if the debates had been public."[5]

The Virginia delegation took the lead and presented the Convention with its first working proposal. This, the Virginia plan, was largely the effort of the thirty-six-year-old Madison, who more than any other person deserves the title "father of the Constitution." He was a short, shy, and soft-spoken man who habitually dressed in black. Madison had not been trained for a profession, but he was widely read, possessed a sharp and questioning mind, and had devoted his life to public service. He understood clearly the historical significance of the meeting of the Convention; it is because he decided to make a detailed private record of the Convention debates that we know so much of what was said that summer in Philadelphia.

This Virginia plan was proposed by Edmund Randolph who, as governor of the state, was titular head of the Virginia delegation; and it was breathtaking. When Randolph moved

25

at the outset that the Convention commit itself to the proposition "that a national government ought to be established consisting of a supreme legislature, judiciary, and executive," the delegates were stunned into silence.[6] They realized that his Virginia plan was to involve more than simply amending the Articles of Confederation. No mere tinkering with the Articles, no more expedients, would suffice any longer. Indeed, Madison's ideas of reform, as he realized, struck "so deeply at the old Confederation, and lead to such a systematic change that they scarcely admit of the expedient."[7] Madison wanted to create a general government that would exercise direct power over individuals and be organized as most of the state governments were organized, with a single executive, a bicameral legislature, and a separate judiciary.

According to the Virginia plan, representation in both houses of the legislature would be proportional to population or to contributions of taxes or to both. The lower house would be elected directly by the people; the upper house would be elected by the lower house from lists of persons nominated by the states. The national executive, the number of which was not specified, would be chosen by the national legislature for a single term of years. The national judiciary, made up of both superior and inferior courts, was to be chosen by the national legislature. The Virginia plan also provided for a council of revision composed of the executive and a number of the national judiciary with a limited veto power over acts of both the national legislature and the state legislatures.

Since the evils of the 1780s flowed from "the turbulence and follies of democracy" within the states, the new government, said Randolph, was to be "a strong *consolidated* union, in which the idea of states should be nearly annihilated."[8] Thus the Virginia plan gave the national legislature the authority to legislate "in all cases to which the states are incompetent" and to veto or "to negative all laws passed by the several States, contravening in the opinion of the National Legislature, the articles of Union."[9] This latter legislature power to negative all state laws contravening the union was in addition to the veto power over state laws given to the proposed council of revision. This double veto of state legislation was a measure of Madison's deep revulsion with what the states had been

26

doing in the 1780s. He thought the national legislature's proposed veto authority over all state legislation "to be absolutely necessary, and to be the least possible encroachment on the State jurisdictions." It would enable the national government to play the same role the English crown had been supposed to play in the British empire—that of a "disinterested umpire" over clashing interests.[10] By a vote of six states to one, the Convention agreed at the outset to make this Virginia plan the basis for its deliberations.

The delegates found it difficult to agree finally on any one thing, because agreement on one part of the government could later be unsettled by changes made in another part. Some, for example, were reluctant to agree on an executive of one person or several persons until they knew the extent of authority the executive would be given. Eventually, however, the Convention agreed on a single executive with power to execute the laws.

But agreement on these sorts of matters could not hide the basic chasm that was opening up as delegates began facing up to the nationalist implications of the Virginia plan. The Virginia plan seemed to some delegates to be too consolidating. It swallowed up the states and ignored their existence and integrity. While nearly all the delegates at Philadelphia were eager to create a stronger central government, some of them soon came to realize that the Virginia plan went too far.

The issue was first raised on June 9 by William Paterson of New Jersey. What bothered Paterson was the Virginia plan's proposal that both houses of the national legislature be proportionally representative. This, said Paterson, would destroy the integrity and sovereignty of each of the states and place majority power in the hands of the representatives from the large states. New Jersey, he warned, would never agree to confederate on these terms. Wilson of Pennsylvania retorted hotly that the people of his state would never confederate if each state was to have equal representation. Two days later, on June 11, the Convention reaffirmed the principle of proportional representation embodied in the Virginia plan, but the vote for proportional representation for the upper house, or what would become the Senate, was close, six states to five.

This vote galvanized the opposition. On June 15, Paterson proposed nine resolutions which became the New Jersey plan.

These were essentially nine amendments to the Articles of Confederation, maintaining the basic structure of the old Confederation with the equal representation of each state in the Congress, but granting to the Congress all the powers of taxation and regulating commerce that many in the 1780s had wanted. New Jersey was supported by the delegates from Connecticut, New York, and Delaware. Paterson and other supporters of the New Jersey plan were not opposed to a strong national government, but, as John Dickinson warned Madison, they thought the Virginia plan was "pushing things too far." As much as they wanted "a good National Government," they would never allow the states to be totally swallowed up.[11] With two such different proposals before it, the Convention was at a crisis.

On June 18, in the midst of this debate over the Virginia and New Jersey plans, Alexander Hamilton of New York suddenly arose and made his own personal proposal for a government in a four- to five-hour-long speech. His proposed government was consolidated to the extreme, virtually abolishing the states as independent entities. He wanted an executive and senate elected for life with the executive to have an absolute veto power. The states remained as mere administrative units with their governors to be appointed by the national government. He accompanied his plan with praise for the English constitution and criticism of the Virginia plan. Although Hamilton's speech has puzzled historians, the timing of it suggests that he probably saw his extreme proposals as a means of making the Virginia plan seem more moderate, a middle-of-the-road compromise between his plan and the New Jersey plan. He certainly went out of his way to lump the Virginia plan together with the New Jersey plan as inadequate to deal with "the violence and turbulence of democratic government." "The Virginia plan," he said, was "pork still, with little change of sauce."[12]

Maybe it worked, for on June 19 the Convention voted for the Virginia plan against the New Jersey plan, seven states to three, with one divided. This was the crucial vote of the Convention. It meant that the basic principle of the Articles was rejected. The new national government was not to be a league of states but a government in its own right. But the struggle over the precise role of the states in this national government was not over. It occupied the Convention in heated debate for over a month. As Luther Martin later recalled, the delegates "were on the verge of dissolution, scarce held together by the strength of a hair."[13]

Historians have often pictured the debate over representation of the states *as states* in the national government as one between the small states and the large states. This is misleading. Madison and Wilson, it is true, were delegates from the large populous states of Virginia and Pennsylvania, but their opposition to equal representation of the states in either branch of the national legislature was not based simply on a parochial concern with the interests of their respective states. Madison and Wilson were more cosmopolitan and far-sighted than that. To them, the issue of the debate was whether or not any semblance of the old Confederation would remain in the new Constitution. These nationalists who believed all the ills of the 1780s flowed from the behavior of the states were worried that any equal representation of the states in the new national legislature would in effect perpetuate the state sovereignty that had vitiated the Confederation. If the Senate should contain equal representation from each state, it would only be a matter of time before the states would overawe and dominate the national government. It was for this reason that the nationalists like Madison and Wilson so vehemently opposed equal representation of the states in the Senate.

The crucial vote was taken on July 16, and the so-called "Connecticut compromise," by which each state secured two senators in the upper house, carried by five states to four, with one divided. Madison was stunned. He did not regard the states' equal representation in the Senate as a "compromise." For him and other nationalists, it was a defeat pure and simple. The states would be allowed back into the national government from which the Virginia plan had banished them. Indeed, the Virginia plan with its broad grant of powers to the national legislature and its veto power over all state laws depended on keeping the states as states out of the national government. With this "compromise," everything had become unhinged.

The Virginia delegation was in disarray, and Randolph proposed that the Convention adjourn temporarily in order to give both sides time to "consider the steps proper to be taken in the present solemn crisis of the business."[14] The next morning, on July 17, the nationalists in the Convention caucused to decide whether they should pull out, but they were divided and nothing was done. As Madison observed, this was tantamount to accepting the equality of votes in the Senate.

This nationalist defeat had implications for the whole Virginia plan, and a series of changes and adjustments in the powers of the legislature, in the nature and election of the executive, and in the authority of the judiciary inevitably followed the "Connecticut compromise."

In place of the broad and indefinite legislative authority granted by the Virginia plan, the Congress was now given a specific list of powers, which became Article I, Section 8 of the final Constitution. And the authority of the legislature to negative all state laws was likewise abandoned, much to Madison's chagrin. In its stead, the Convention presented a series of prohibitions on the states, which became Article I, Section 10 of the Constitution. The states were forbidden among other things to levy customs duties on imports or exports, to enter into treaties, to coin money, to emit paper money, and to pass bills of attainder, ex post facto laws, or laws impairing contracts. These prohibitions were serious. Not only were they directed at the principal legislative vices of the 1780s, but they in effect promised to make the states nearly economically incompetent. In that premodern world, customs duties were the most common and efficient form of taxation. Now with the Constitution the states would lose not only this major source of taxes but also the capacity to print paper money—something that had carried the colonies and states through numerous wars in the eighteenth century. At a stroke, the Constitution prohibited what the British government in its various currency laws had earlier tried to do.

Madison did not easily accept the loss of the national legislature's negative over state laws. Without it, he told Jefferson in the early fall of 1787, the Constitution would not answer its purposes: it would neither solve the national problems "nor prevent the local mischiefs which everywhere excite disgusts against the state governments."[15] Madison had little confidence in the suggestion made by some that the national judiciary might be able to keep the state legislatures within bounds. Several of the delegates were, indeed, coming to count on the judiciary more and more. Early on the Convention had rejected Madison's plan for a joint executive-judicial council of revision with a limited veto power over both national and state legislation. Most of the delegates thought that the judges by themselves could set aside unconstitutional laws and ought not to be mixed up in the passing of these laws. And despite the persistent efforts of Madison and other nationalists to revive this council of revision, the decision to have the judiciary stand alone held. Although many of the delegates glimpsed that the Supreme Court would have the capacity to declare unconstitutional laws void, none of them clearly anticipated the lengths this power of the judiciary to review legislation would eventually be carried.

Far more attention was paid to the executive. Originally the executive, like the governors in the states, was to have only restricted powers. Though he was granted a limited veto power over acts of Congress and was made commander-in-chief of the armed forces, the Committee of Detail at first gave to the Senate exclusively the power of appointment of ambassadors and justices of the Supreme Court and the power to make treaties. But once Madison and other nationalists thought through the implications of state influence in the Senate following the "compromise" of July 16, they chose to place these powers in the hands of the President with the Senate advising and consenting only.

The "compromise" of July 16 also affected the mode of electing the President. If he were elected by the whole Congress including a Senate in which the states would have equal representation, it was feared that he might become a captive of state interests. To avoid this and to keep the executive independent of the legislature, some suggested a single seven-year term for the President without the right of re-election. Others like James Wilson wanted the President elected directly by the people. But others feared that the huge size of the nation would in the future (after Washington) prevent the people's knowing who the best men were. Finally, after much discussion and many votes, the Convention hit upon the electoral college. It combined most of what the delegates wanted and did so without the deficiences of the various proposals. It removed the choice of the President from the Congress and thus assured his independence without limiting the number of terms he could serve. Yet at the same time the electoral college was an exact replica of Congress, and thus had all the advantages of the July 16 "compromise" on representation between the nationally-minded and the small states. Many expected the electoral college to work as a nominating body in which no one usually would get a majority of electoral votes; therefore, most elections would take place in the House of Representatives among the top five candidates with each state's congressional delegation voting as a unit. The electoral college was an ingenious solution to delicate and controversial political problems, and the fact that it has rarely worked as it was originally intended takes none of its ingeniousness away.[16]

In the end, Madison and other nationalists were very pessimistic about the Constitution. As a remedy for the ills of the 1780s, it fell short of the mark. Still, it was better than the Articles of Confederation, and Madison and Hamilton and others began working actively to secure ratification by the states. In the Constitution, wrote Madison, "we behold a republican remedy for the diseases most incident to republican government."[17]

But why? Why was the new federal government more able to deal with the vices of the system than the states? Why should this national government be trusted and the states not trusted? In what ways was it different from the state governments? Madison, for one, saw the relevance of these questions. "It may be asked," he said, "how private rights will be more secure under the Guardianship of the General Government than under the State governments, since they are both founded in the republican principle which refers the ultimate decision to the will of the majority."[18] What, in other words, would keep the new national government from succumbing to the same popular pressures that had afflicted the state governments and had created the problems of democracy in the states?

The answer given to these questions by the supporters of the Constitution, or the Federalists as they called themselves, reveals their social perspective. They believed they could trust the national government more than the state governments

32

because they expected different sorts of men to sit in the national government from those who sat in the state governments. Much of the problem of majoritarian factionalism and populist politics in the state legislatures came from the kinds of people getting elected to these legislatures. Too many of what the Federalists thought were obscure ordinary men with "factious tempers" and "localist prejudices," men like Abraham Yates, a part-time lawyer and shoemaker of Albany and William Findley, a Scotch Irish ex-weaver of Pittsburgh, were bypassing traditional gentry leadership and using demogogic skills to get elected to the state legislatures.[19]

The Federalists hoped that the elevated nature of the new national government would keep such factious and narrow-minded men out of government and allow more educated, more cosmopolitan, and more enlightened sorts of men to hold office. Madison called the process by which this would take place one of "filtration." By enlarging the electorate and decreasing the number of representatives, the new federal structure would ensure that better sorts of men would be elected, "men who possess the most attractive merit and the most diffusive and established characters."[20] The five congressmen from North Carolina in the new government, for example, were more apt to be more respectable and enlightened than the 232 who sat in the North Carolina legislature. The first House of Representatives in the Congress provided for only 65 members; these few were more likely to be more educated and more cosmopolitan than the hundreds of men who were in the various state legislatures. Or so the Federalists hoped.

No one tried to work out the intellectual and theoretical implications of the new government more thoroughly or more consistently than did James Madison. Madison turned the traditional assumptions about republicanism on their head. Instead of agreeing with Montesquieu that a republic had to be small in size and homogeneous in interests, Madison borrowed an insight from David Hume and argued that a republic was actually most suited to large territory with a heterogeneity of interests. "What remedy can be found in a republican Government, where the majority must ultimately decide," Madison argued, "but that of giving such an extent to its sphere, that no one common interest or passion will be likely to unite a majority of the whole number in an unjust pursuit."[21] The large extent and the elevated nature of the new national government was the best way of dealing with democratic passions and interests.

But Madison did not expect the new national government to have no common interest or no public good to promote. Madison was not an originator of what is now called an "interest-group" or "pluralist" conception of politics. Despite his hardheaded appreciation of the prevalence of interests in politics, he did not believe that public policy or the common good would emerge naturally from the give-and-take of hosts of competing interests. Instead, he hoped that these clashing interests and factions in an enlarged national republic would neutralize themselves and thereby allow liberally educated, rational men, "whose enlightened views and virtuous sentiments render them superior to local prejudices and to schemes of injustice," to promote the public good in a disinterested manner.[22] It worked that way in religion. The multiplicity of religious sects in America prevented any one from dominating and thus permitted the enlightened reason of philosophers like Madison and Jefferson to shape public policy and church-state relations.

The opponents of the Constitution, the Antifederalists as they were labelled, saw very clearly what Madison and the Federalists were up to. But instead of seeing enlightened patriots simply making a Constitution to promote the national interest, they saw groups of interested gentry trying to foist an "'aristocracy" onto republican America. And they attacked the Constitution for being an aristocratic document that created a government designed to benefit the few at the expense of the many. In state after state, the Antifederalists reduced the issue to those social terms that the Federalists themselves had created; the Constitution, they charged, was "a continual exertion of the *well-born* of America to obtain that darling domination which they have not been able to accomplish in their respective states." The offices of government, they said, were "too high and exalted to be filled but [by] the *first men* in the State in point of Fortune and Influence," and ordinary local-minded men would be excluded from national politics.[23]

So serious and widespread were the Antifederalist charges that the Constitution was aristocratic and unrepublican that

34

the Federalists were hard put to defend its republican character. Which is why "Publius" in the *Federalist* papers spent so much time demonstrating how republican the new government was.

Still, despite considerable opposition in many of the states to the Constitution, its eventual ratification seemed almost inevitable. The Articles of Confederation were now dead. It was scarcely conceivable that the Confederation Congress could be reassembled. The alternative to the Constitution seemed to be governmental chaos or the fragmentation of the United States into several Confederations. Many who wanted to keep the union but not the Constitution found themselves forced, as Richard Henry Lee complained, to accept "this or nothing."[24]

Many of the small states—Delaware, New Jersey, Connecticut, and Georgia—commercially dependent on their neighbors or militarily exposed, ratified immediately. The critical struggles took place in the large states of Massachusetts, Virginia, and New York. These states accepted the Constitution only by narrow margins and the promise of future amendments. North Carolina and Rhode Island rejected the Constitution, but after New York's ratification in July 1788 the country was ready to go ahead and organize the new government without them. The New York ratification illustrates the Antifederalists' dilemma. Melancthon Smith was the most vigorous and articulate of the New York opponents of the Constitution, but in the end he voted for it. His fear of disunion eventually overcame his fear of the Constitution.

One of the promises the Federalists in some of the state ratifying conventions made to the Antifederalists was the addition of some amendments to the Constitution—a bill of rights. It had soon become obvious to some of the Federalists that the omission of a bill of rights—a declaration of individual rights against the government—made the Constitution very vulnerable to criticism. Such bills of rights had been included in many of the state constitutions, and the federal Constitution's lack of such a major declaration of rights seemed a major political error. Although Jefferson gave a qualified approval of the new government, he was upset that it did not contain a bill of rights. "A bill of rights," he told Madison "is what the people are entitled to against every government on earth, general or particular, and what no just government should refuse, or rest on inference."[25]

Actually, the Philadelphia Convention had scarcely discussed a bill of rights. Only during the final moments of the Convention did George Mason, author of the Virginia declaration of rights, bring the issue up, and it was voted down by every state. Most of the Federalists thought that a national government of delegated powers made a traditional bill of rights irrelevant. But the extent of Antifederalist concern for this omission combined with Jefferson's public stand in favor of a bill of rights eventually forced the Federalists to give way.

Madison, the leader in the new House of Representatives convened in 1789, immediately sought to fulfill promises that had been made to Antifederalists in the ratifying conventions. He beat back Antifederalists' efforts to change fundamentally the provisions of the Constitution and extracted from the variety of suggested amendments those that were least likely to drain energy from the new government. To the disappointment of some Antifederalists, the bill of rights—the ten amendments that were ratified in 1791—were mostly concerned with protecting from the federal government the rights of *individuals* rather than the rights of the *states*. Only the Tenth Amendment, which reserved for the states or the people those powers not delegated to the United States, was a concession to the main Antifederalist fear that the federal government would swallow up the states. Thus even the bill of rights that had begun as an Antifederalist weapon ended up in the Federalists' hands. The Constitution was launched amid great expectations and high hopes.

Of course, the Constitution and the new federal government did not develop quite the way the Founders had anticipated; few things in history ever do. But the fact that the Constitution did not fulfill all of the Founders' hopes and expectations should be gratifying to us. It makes the Founders seem more fallible, more human, and helps to close that terrifying gap that exists between them and us. They may not have been as insecure and uncertain of the future as we are, but despite the myths, they were not demi-gods and the Constitution was not a miracle. It was without doubt a monumental political act, but it did not solve many of the political problems its creators expected it to solve. Much remained, and still remains, for the future.

NOTES FOR LECTURE II

1. *Letters from the Federal Farmer to the Republican* (1787-88), ed. Walter Hartwell Bennett (University, Alabama: University of Alabama Press, 1978), 6-7.
2. Boston, *Massachusetts Centinel*, May 19, 1787; Madison to Edmund Randolph, April 2, 1787, in Hutchinson et al., eds., *Papers of Madison*, IX, 362.
3. Washington to Hamilton, 1 September 1796, Fitzpatrick, ed., *Writings of Washington*, XXXV, 199-200.
4. Henry, quoted in Max Farrand, *The Framing of the Constitution* (New Haven: Yale University Press, 1913), 15.
5. Gordon S. Wood, "The Democratization of Mind in the American Revolution," in Robert H. Horwitz, ed., *The Moral Foundations of the American Republic* (Charlottesville, Virginia: University Press of Virginia, 1986), 122.
6. Max Farrand, ed., *The Records of the Federal Convention of 1787* (New Haven: Yale University Press, 1911, 1937), I, 41.
7. Madison, quoted in Wood, *Creation of American Republic*, 473.
8. Farrand, ed., *Records*, I, 51, 24.
9. Farrand, ed., *Records*, I, 21.
10. Madison to Washington, 16 April 1787, Hutchinson et al., eds., *Papers of Madison*, IX, 383, 384.
11. Farrand, ed., *Records*, I, 242.
12. Farrand, ed., *Records*, I, 282-293.
13. Luther Martin, quoted by Warren, *Making of the Constitution*, 309.
14. Farrand, ed., *Records*, II, 18.
15. Madison to Jefferson, 6 Septembr 1787, in Julian P. Boyd, ed., *The Papers of Thomas Jefferson* (Princeton: Princeton University Press, 1955), XII, 103.
16. On the creation of the Electoral College see Shlomo Slonim, "The Electoral College at Philadelphia: The Evolution of an Ad Hoc Congress for the Selection of a President," *The Journal of American History*, 73 (1986), 35-58.
17. *The Federalist*, No. 10.
18. Madison to Jefferson, 24 October 1787, in Boyd, ed., *Papers of Jefferson*, XII, 276.

19. *The Federalist,* No. 10.
20. *The Federalist,* No. 10.
21. Madison to Jefferson, 24 October 1787, in Boyd, ed., *Papers of Jefferson,* XII, 278.
22. *The Federalist,* No. 10.
23. Wood, *Creation of American Republic,* 514, 515.
24. Lee to George Mason, 1 October 1787, in James Curtis Ballagh, ed., *The Letters of Richard Henry Lee* (New York: Da Capo Press, 1914), II, 438.
25. Jefferson to Madison, 20 December 1787, in Boyd, ed., *Papers of Jefferson,* XII, 440.

GORDON S. WOOD

Dr. Gordon S. Wood, professor of American history at Brown University, was born in Concord, Massachusetts, on November 27, 1933. He graduated summa cum laude and Phi Beta Kappa from Tufts University in 1955. After three years in the United States Air Force, he earned the A.M. and Ph.D. degrees from Harvard University.

A specialist in Colonial American and Early National history, Professor Wood taught at William and Mary (1964-1966), Harvard (1966-1967), and the University of Michigan (1967-1969) before joining the faculty at Brown. In 1982-1983 he served as Pitt Professor of American History at Cambridge University, England, and from 1983 to 1986 he chaired the Department of History at Brown.

Professor Wood has written *Representation in the American Revolution* (1969), *The Creation of the American Republic* (1969), *Revolution and the Political Integration of the Enslaved and Disfranchised* (1974), and *Social Radicalism and Equality in the American Revolution* (1976). He is co-author of *The Great Republic* (1977), and has edited *The Rising Glory of America, 1760-1820* (1971) and *The Confederation and the Constitution* (1973).

He has contributed selections to numerous anthologies and collective works including *Leadership in the American Revolution*(1974), *We Americans* (1975), *The Book of the States* (1976), *New Directions in American Intellectual History* (1979), *How Democratic is the Constitution?* (1980), *The Constitution and the Budget* (1980), and *This Constitution: Our Enduring Legacy* (1986).

Also, Professor Wood has published a number of articles in scholarly and popular journals,, among them the *William and Mary Quarterly*, *New England Quarterly*, *Brown Alumni Magazine*, *New York History*, and *National Forum*.

Professor Wood's scholarship and teaching have won him the De Lancey K. Jay Prize (1963-1964) and the Toppan Prize (1964) from Harvard University, the John H. Dunning Prize from the American Historical Association (1970), the Bancroft Prize from Columbia University (1970), the Kerr Prize from the New York Historical Society (1981), and the Douglass Adair Award (1984).

Although teaching and writing are his primary interests, Professor Wood has served his profession in a variety of capacities. He has been a member of the fellowship committe of the American Antiquarian Society, the American Historical Committee for the Bicentennial Celebration of the American Revolution, the Program Committee of the Organization of American Historians, the Merle Curti Book Award Committe of the Organization of American Historians, the Board of Editors of the *Journal of American History* and *Eighteenth Century Studies*, and the Board of Advisors of the History Book Club, the National Historical Society, and the Society for Historians of the Early Republic. He is currently president of the Society of Historians of the Early Republic.

Previous
CHARLES EDMONDSON HISTORICAL LECTURES

1977-78
Paul K. Conkin, *American Christianity in Crisis*: "Religious Rationalism—God without a Redeemer" and "Darwinism—Nature without a Creator" (Baylor University Press)

1979-80
Walter LaFeber, *The Third Cold War*: "The Kissinger Response" and "The Carter Response" (Baylor University Press)

1980-81
Martin E. Marty, *Religious Crises in Modern America*: "The Modernist Attraction, 1880-1925" and "The Fundamentalist Attraction, 1925-1980" (Baylor University Press)

1981-82
William H. McNeill, *The Great Frontier: Freedom and Hierarchy in Modern Times* (Princeton University Press)

1982-83
Robert L. Heilbroner, "Capitalism in Transition: The Twenty-first Century"

1983-84
C. Vann Woodward, "Continuing Themes in Southern History: The Strange Career of Jim Crow, 1954-1984" and "The Burden of Southern History, 1952-1984"

1984-85
William E. Leuchtenburg, *The 1984 Election in Historical Perspective*: "From the Civil War to the New Deal" and "Toward a New Party System" (Baylor University Press)

1985-86
Peter Gay, *Aggression: A Historian's Theme in Search of a Theory*: "Toward a Theory of Aggression" and "Humor: Aggression at Work"

Breinigsville, PA USA
27 September 2010
246170BV00001B/2/A